KEVIN PRICE Christmas 1973

DAVID COLEMAN'S
WORLD
OF
FOOTBALL

Reporter: Norman Harris

PURNELL London

Contents

Wolves refuse to submit

By ...

gave Par... ...
It had been an exciting
game so far and the
Wolves fans were given
another treat when
Dougan rushed in to meet
a cross on the right,
but fortunately Lloyd was
on hand to deflect the
ball clear.

... lost an ...
... before the ha...
... caught it.
...ost matches are tilted ...mid-
...defiant on the right and Holland, ...ter).

...alternate... tim... and
Referee.—R. Matthewson (Manches-

...was firmly hoiste...
...where Perryman's...
...and Peters's per...
...especially importa...
...outstanding goalke...
...son, who had save...
...Peters in the thir...
...in the end ...
...Tottenham ...

LIVERPOOL'S one moment of joy. Kevin Keegan sweeps on to John Toshack's headed pass and hammers in an

Wolves warning in title chase

Wolves 2, Liverpool 1—by ...

WOLVES, who have been
struggling to find their
true form for most of the
season finally managed it
— with a patched-up
team against the First
Division leaders.

And b... ...eir won
deserv... ...

strength ...nd raking
accurat... ...res plus the
c... ...

That H... ...
...

CLEMENCE STRANDED

Sunderland crossed from
the right, Dougan headed it
back across the box where
McCalliog could not quite
reach the ball.

HUGHES turned to push
it back to Clemence and,
with the goalkeeper
stranded, it just beat the
retreating Liverpool
defenders over the line.

Liverpool equalised in the
17th minute with their first
serious attack on the Wolves
goal.

Munro lost the ball to
Toshack who hit it across the
goal for KEEGAN to hammer
past Parkes from 12 yards.

A minute later and a
Wagstaffe cross had Lloyd
heading for a corner as
Richards tried to beat him to
...tre.

THREATEN

PAID OFF!

The pressure Wolves were
putting on Liverpool just had
to pay off and in the 78th
minute RICHARDS put them
ahead with a finely worked
goal initiated by Shaw who
had really played well in mid-
field.

Result
WOLVES 2, LIVERPOOL 1.
Gold...

That decision infuriated the home fans who were further incensed when Lloyd halted a Dougan breakaway with a sort of clumsy rugby tackle.

Lloyd was booked for that incident and has since been heavily criticised, but in defence of the centre half it did seem to me that as the two started to chase a through ball, old fox Dougan held Lloyd back before beginning to outpace him.

The fact remains that the Liverpool defence as a whole had a bad time, and twice in the opening

Though Heighway, Keegan and Toshack all flickered briefly, Liverpool were incapable of applying the sustained pressure that has crushed opponents in the past, and there was a distinct uneasiness in defence, where Smith and Lloyd struggled against the harrying Dougan and Richards. Dougan, though his is more of a secondary role to the youthful and rapidly improving Richards these days, is still playing a useful part in Wolves' attacking plays.

The game erupted in the 60th minute when there was a flare-up between Lloyd and Dougan. A long clearance from the Wolves penalty area was mis-judged by Lloyd, and as it bounced past him, Dougan ran on, with only Clemence to beat — but Lloyd pulled him down.

The referee had no hesitation in taking Lloyd's name.

Football

Liverpool's pursuers ought to take heart from manner of defeat

By Tom

ut it wasn't enough.

Dougan's Match

This is what any football spectator would like to be able to do: to discuss the game he has just seen with one of its leading players. This is what happened after the Wolves v. Liverpool match of last season. The spectator — a completely neutral one — was John Bentley, a teacher from Bromley, Kent. The player was Derek Dougan of Wolves. This is the record of their conversation.

Bentley: Why do you think you won, in general?

Dougan: Well, we haven't been playing very well at home, we were overdue. And Liverpool, top of the League you know—they're scalps worth having. The crowd was 33,000, about 9,000 above average. All this helps. In fact, in the six years I've been playing for Wolves, in 12 matches against Liverpool that probably is our most effective display.

Bentley: For me, the score seemed a pretty fair reflection. For all their skills, Liverpool never really controlled any part of the game, they seemed harried by Wolves' running.

Dougan: Probably the decisive factor in the game was the speed of Richards and myself. We're probably the quickest pair of front runners in the game. But you see, the player we rely on, and have done now for two years or more, is David Wagstaffe, and he's been struggling a bit. This was only his eleventh appearance in 27 games. Now, provided we got the proper service, we knew before the match that we could outrun their back two men. The way they play, Smith and Lloyd take the two front runners. Well, we like to get them in a position where we can exploit them with a little bit of pace and with crosses. In the first half two marvellous crosses came across and Larry Lloyd just got a touch on two of them to touch them away, and I was behind him for both of those. It's typical of our game really. But there are certain key positions, and if we had someone like Wagstaffe on the right side . . .

Bentley: I thought the Wolves play revolved very much around the two players of Munro at the back and Richards up front. It seemed to me that Munro controlled the defence and marshalled the whole team.

Dougan: Yes, Frank's a very useful footballer. But young Richards—there's no question about this—twelve months ago they said he was full of potential and he's fulfilled his potential now and John Richards is a very good front runner indeed.

Bentley: And you, Derek, you were winning the ball so easily, it seemed to me. For all his height, Lloyd was either having to climb on your back or you were finding the room you needed.

Dougan: Well, you see, with the likes of Larry Lloyd, what happens is this. There's no doubt that with dead-ball kicks or kicks from the goalkeeper the defender should be favourite. And while there's only two defenders in the League as big as myself—Larry Lloyd and Mike England—what I do against them is this. When the ball is, like, dropping, I go up to take it but then I go back, so that I go into him, because I know that if I just stand and wait he's going to come into me. Well, five times out of ten it works. Either I get the touch or I get it down onto my chest, or I get a foul for him impeding me—really, when it's half-a-dozen of one and six of the other. But generally, I like these aerial clashes with the big fellows. It's a shame that time's running out on me.

Bentley: I get the impression from looking at the Wolves side that you've got too many average players.

Dougan: Well, I'm glad that *you* said that. They can rise to the occasion like they did today.

Bentley: Yes, they did. They rose to the occasion in the second half but in the first half they were lacking, and I got the impression that Liverpool were coming back into the game and were holding their own. But generally speaking, Liverpool were disappointing in mid-field.

Dougan: I thought they were not only disappointing—with the exception of Lindsay, and Clemence, I thought they all played below par. It's just one of those particular days. After all, it's away from home. Last week they dropped a point at home—the first point they dropped at home for almost two years. In fact, they don't score many goals away from home. We realise that, and in fact I was saying to my next-door neighbour today, I said, 'If there is a score there won't be many goals today'.

Bentley: You seem to use a lot of high balls into the middle. It was not until you used Wagstaffe that you got into the game.

Dougan: Well, it's rather easy to say that about pumping the high balls up. There are often so many people in midfield that you've got to knock the ball over the top. Sometimes it's the distribution by the people who are knocking it around that spoils it. But look at the game. The most exciting high ball of the game was the ball that went over Lloyd's head and he had to pull me down.

Bentley: He really did drag you down. What did he have to say about it?

Dougan: He said, 'I had to do it'. And I said, 'Yes, you're right. You did.'

Bentley: I liked the way that instead of getting angry you just looked down at your jersey and plucked at it to see if it was still in shape. And then walked well away.

Dougan: Well, I was thinking about my award as the best-dressed footballer! I wanted to make sure my shirt wasn't ruffled . . . But no, getting angry only makes matters worse. I wasn't angry anyway. I save all my energy now for the game.

Bentley: What about Steve Heighway? He wasn't in the game at all really. I thought he was actually the quickest and most positive player on the field. But in the second half, he only touched the ball about seven times.

Dougan: Did he? Well, you find that happens sometimes.

Bentley: He seemed to be playing all over the front of the Liverpool offence, perhaps they couldn't find him.

Dougan: I think that Steve Heighway's particular strength is in playing on the left side. He's very quick, and he gets this sort of change of feet, like the Muhammed Ali shuffle, and he goes to turn this way and that way, and then he gets down the left side, crosses the ball, and there's no doubt that this Toshack is very dangerous near the far post. And he never had much of it in the game, with the exception of the equaliser that they knocked across. They knocked it across to Toshack and across the goal and, due credit to Keegan, he put it in well. I think that Keegan's a very fortunate young man in the fact that he's playing in such a strong side as Liverpool, otherwise I don't think he'd be the jewel that he's made out to be.

Dougan pulled down by Lloyd . . . A brouhaha develops, while Lloyd goes down, apparently injured . . . Dougan walks clear of the argument

Bentley: Yes, Keegan gets a lot of good service. The ball pushed into his stride easily.

Dougan: Well, yes. He's really the unorthodox player of the side.

Bentley: I liked Lindsay's game today.

Dougan: Yes, I like Alec Lindsay. He's got a beautiful left peg. And Chris Lawler, he's a very classy full back, I've admired his play for a long long time.

Bentley: I thought the game today was a very clean game. Apart from that trouble you had with Smith, when he knocked you down and then you held on to his boot, and ended up ruffling his hair.

Dougan: Yes. You see, Tommy Smith's another one. I've always said this about Tommy Smith, that if you cut his tongue out, he couldn't play. Tremendous talker, and that's what it's all about. Dave Mackay was like that. You find that players who do good jobs for you at the back, they're always tremendous talkers.

Bentley: Why do you think that Bill Shankly behaves like this after a game and bundles his team straight off into the coach and away? I don't know what I'd think about that if I was a player.

Dougan: Well, hell, I think most managers behave like that. I know Bill Shankly very well and I adore the man. I can only give him the highest praise. In this case our players were talking about it after the match — it's the first time in their lives as professional footballers that the other manager, coming

13

up the passage, has said 'Well done lads, you played well'. They have never known this before. It takes a bloody big man to say that. And there's no doubt that he's a very professional man, and it's better that he gets it out of his system now whatever he's got to say, rather than brood over the night and over the weekend.

Bentley: What do you think Shankly's going to say to them?

Dougan: Well, you see, there's not much really a manager can say.

Bentley: There wasn't a lack of commitment?

Dougan: No, no. You see, when you set such high standards for yourself, it's very difficult to keep up to them all the time.

Bentley: What about your own manager, Bill McGarry? What did he have to say?

Dougan: Bill McGarry was delighted. He's not often delighted, he's a very hard man to please.

Bentley: He seemed fairly quiet when I saw him walking around before and after the game. There was not much emotion evident.

Dougan: Yes, Bill McGarry's very good at hiding emotion. At his own place, he really can have a go at the players. He's a manager who really has a go so verbally, full-time and half-time. He's another man who can't keep it inside himself, and it's a good thing.

Bentley: Did he speak to you at half-time?

Dougan: Yes, he did, but he always seems to say the right thing. He said, 'If we keep on . . .' Actually he was very annoyed — he thought the defence should have cut out the equaliser. He didn't give them the benefit of the doubt saying, well, it may have been offside. He just said it should have been cut out. Then he went on to say that if we keep it up and keep on running about, reiterating that if you're fit and in good condition there's nothing to stop you from going and going out there. You won't drop dead. Hard work's never killed anybody.

Bentley: Yes, they really began to run in the second half, particularly Shaw and Sunderland. Are they youngsters in the team?

Dougan: Bernard Shaw — well, he'll probably kill me for saying this, but he's probably the oldest teenager in Wolverhampton. Alan Sunderland, he's about 19. Now he's another one. If he believes in himself . . .

Bentley: They were saying in the crowd as I was coming away after the game that even Wolves with a makeshift side, as they had today, could beat anybody.

Dougan: Yes. There again, you see, Kenny Hibbitt, he's not been playing well. He asked to be left out. And I admire that. I admire a player being honest. There's no doubt that sometimes players can play themselves out of a bad rut — but anyway, he's playing in the Reserves today. But you see, these other players, they're not overawed by the occasion, because they're training every day. It's not exactly strange to them.

Bentley: Watching your play, what is obvious is the considerable experience that you benefit from.

Derek Dougan: Replacing his replacements.

Dougan: Yes, well, plus the fact that I've still got that turn of speed—which is very essential for a front runner. Plus the fact that I know the opposition inside out. I don't have to think about it any more.

Bentley: You said that time is running out for you. How long do you think you've got left in League soccer?

Dougan: Well, if I've got another twelve months or two years in the First Division, I'll be delighted.

Bentley: They were saying in the crowd while I was talking to them that Dougan couldn't play in the Reserves. That is, it was going to be First Division football, or out.

Dougan: Yes, that's it. That's how it will be, and I think everyone realises that.

Bentley: Do you think they're going to start substituting you?

Dougan: The manager is very good to me at the moment. I've got a good understanding. And I've said to the manager, that if he wants to buy another player, that's fair enough. I understand that. But the trouble is, Curran's come and gone. Bobby Gould's gone. Young Peter Eastoe, the youth international, I thought he was going to make the grade, but he's playing in the Reserves and he hasn't made the progress that I thought he was going to make as yet. If he could find another couple of inches, or get an extra yard from somewhere, he'd make another front runner . . . The trouble is, really, that in the last four years I've replaced all my replacements!

15

Pictures
of the Year

DCWF

In the Air

Above: Peter Osgood of Chelsea outjumps Arsenal's Frank McLintock.
Right: Joicey of Sheffield Wednesday heads towards the Hull goal.

18

Above: Arsenal's Charlie George and Beattie of Ipswich.
Right: Mid-air duel between Beal of Spurs and Bremner of Leeds.

In the Air

Charlie George for Arsenal beats Newcastle's Moncur.

Conroy of Stoke beneath Kinnear of Spu

Clash

Right: Alan Ball of Arsenal and Billy Bremner of Leeds. Below: Alan Ball and Chelsea's Ron Harris. Below right: Mike England and Peter Osgood fight for the ball.

Punch-out

A scramble in the Hayes goal.

Newcastle's goal-keeper McFaul punches clear an Arsenal attack.

Arsenal and Coventry players in the Arsenal goalmouth.

Confrontation

Clyde Best of West Ham, versus West Bromwich.

Bremner of Leeds, versus Coventry.

Left: Paul Reaney of Leeds tackles John Hughes of Crystal Palace. Below: Munro of Wolves and Clyde Best of West Ham in action. Right: Derby's John O'Hare tackled by Chelsea's Ron Harris.

Confrontation

Thomas of Queen's Park Rangers, and Burnley defenders.

Disputation

Boersma of Liverpool, and Leeds defence.

Madeley and Steve Kindon in a tussle.

Disputation

Arsenal's Bob McNab is tackled by Leicester's Farringdon.

Battle of the Cheque Book

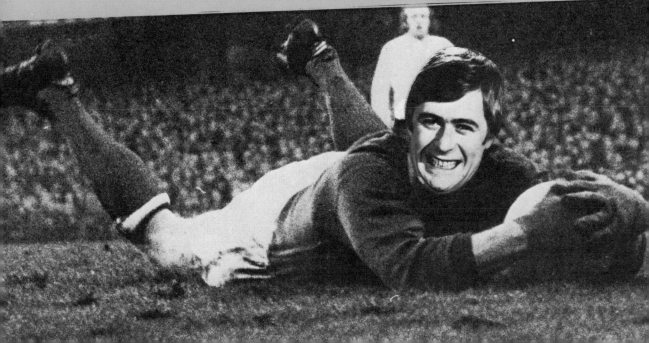

At left, Eric Morecambe turns a shot around the near post. Below, Mike Yarwood anxiously seizes a loose ball. As a result of their outstanding form in goal, each has been given the No.1 shirt in teams which they select from the best players (of any nationality) playing in the English League. This is a game that anyone can play in their own home — perhaps, more successfully than Morecambe and Yarwood? First each of them, independently, selects the 10 men to play in front of him, and puts a price beside each. Each 'selector' has two million pounds to spend. The minimum price they can offer for a player is £100,000. First, Morecambe* and Yarwood** agree on a pool of 20 players from which to make their selections. The 20 players are:

McFarland (Derby County), England (Spurs), Todd (Derby), Bobby Moore (West Ham), Hunter (Leeds), Hughes (Liverpool), Storey (Arsenal), Madeley (Leeds), Giles (Leeds), Bremner (Leeds), Bell (Man. City), Ball (Arsenal), Lorimer (Leeds), Clarke (Leeds), Chivers (Spurs), Channon (Southampton), Marsh (Man. City), Heighway (Liverpool), Macdonald (Newcastle), Ian Moore (Man. United).

FIRST CHOICE FOR
MORECAMBE AND YARWOOD

Eric Morecambe

Todd £350,000	McFarland £150,000	England £100,000		Hunter £150,000
	Marsh £200,000			Madeley £150,000
Lorimer £150,000	Macdonald £250,000	Clarke £250,000	Ian Moore £200,000	

an Moore £100,000	Heighway £150,000	Chivers £150,000	Marsh £200,000	Ball £100,000
Bobby Moore £100,000		McFarland £200,000		Bremner £120,000
Todd £120,000				Madeley £100,000

Mike Yarwood

*Director, Luton Town

**President, Stockport County

The two selectors have clashed on five players. First, McFarland. Morecambe has nominated £150,000 to Yarwood's £200,000. McFarland goes to Yarwood, and Morecambe crosses him off. Now, Todd?

Yarwood: A hundred and twenty thousand.

Morecambe: Three hundred and fifty thousand.

Three hundred and fifty?!

Morecambe: He's the best player in Britain.

Now, the clash over Madeley

Morecambe: I've got Madeley playing in the old-fashioned position of left half.

Yarwood: I've got Madeley as a right fullback.

Morecambe: Have you really?

Yarwood: Yes I have.

Morecambe: He'll be happy about that!

Yarwood: I've got him playing at No. 2 at the back, next to Glenda Jackson. Because I thought Eric would. (laughter)

For Madeley, Morecambe has paid £150,000, Yarwood £100,000. Morecambe gets another player. Now the clash over the two forwards, Ian Moore and Marsh. First, Ian Moore?

Morecambe: Two hundred thousand.
Yarwood: One hundred.

Another signing for Morecambe. Now, Marsh?

Morecambe: Two hundred thousand.
Yarwood: The same: Two hundred.

Marsh will have to be bartered for.

Yarwood: Well, I would certainly, er, have to . . . (Brian Clough voice) He's a hell of a player, a *hell* of a player . . . I'll have to put another fifty thousand on.

Morecambe: (also Clough voice) Well, I will say, I would go up another fifty thousand, which would make Marsh three hundred thousand for me.

Yarwood: Three hundred and fifty thousand.

Morecambe: Well I can't do that. So you've got Marsh.

Morecambe has to fill his 'lost' places, McFarland at the back, and Marsh.

Morecambe: I'll take Storey to replace McFarland, and I'll have Channon for Marsh. That's £175,000 each. And that's me fully paid up.

Now Yarwood, to replace Madeley, Todd and Ian Moore.

Yarwood: I'll take Storey, to replace McFarland. I'll pay £190,000.

And in place of Ian Moore?

Yarwood: Emlyn Hughes.

Hughes? Ian Moore is a winger.

Yarwood: Correct.

Morecambe: Will Mr Moore . . . will Mr Ian Moore please stand up!

Yarwood: No, Emlyn Hughes to play in place of Colin Todd. I'll pay £200,000 for Hughes.

And for the No. 11 shirt, in place of Moore?

Yarwood: Colin Bell.

And Morecambe's replacement for Storey?

Morecambe: Difficult, isn't it? Let's think now . . . Well, I'll have to put in Bremner out of position . . . But's he's got Bremner hasn't he? And he's got Hughes. And I've got Hunter already . . . Alright, then, I'll take Todd from right-half and put him at fullback. And I'll bring in Giles at right-half.

Both selectors consider their team. They're both happy with the teams?

Morecambe: Against Luton, I'd have no worries.

Yarwood: I'd be happy with Luton *Reserves* at Edgely Park, Stockport.

They both chose Rodney Marsh, yet Marsh was the one player that Ramsey dropped?

Morecambe: I think, personally, that Marsh was made a scapegoat. He's got it, you know.

Yarwood: He lives near me, you know.
Morecambe: He'll do anything for a laugh.

Yarwood: He does, actually. I was with him the other week, at City, and gave him a lift home. He had a great game. He is an exciting player.

Morecambe: That's right. I remember when he was down at QPR. I've seen him at Luton, I've had chats with him, I find him a charming boy. I think he is liable to over-act in the penalty box, but maybe as he gets older he'll get over that. But I'd love to see him with Macdonald and Clarke in a line-up. I think that would be fabulous.

From a Cog in the Machine to a Marked Man

ALAN MULLERY started his League career with Fulham. Two years ago he went back to them on loan from Tottenham Hotspur, where he was unhappy at not regaining a first-team place after injury. After six games for Fulham, Spurs needed him back again, to help out in the EUFA Cup. Mullery's previously sad story became a triumph, as he scored a vital goal against Inter-Milan in the away-leg of the semi-final, and then again in the final at Tottenham. It might have been expected that Mullery would now stay at Tottenham, his club for 10 years, but he went back to Fulham. Those were his wishes. Although in most people's minds he had been briefly on loan to Fulham, in his mind he had been on loan back to Tottenham. This last season at Craven Cottage was his first, full season in the Second Division for 12 years. The England wing-half, the man who marked Pele so tigerishly in Mexico, enjoyed himself immensely.

The first time, they were struggling, they were bottom of the Second Division, so every game was crucial. And the teams we were playing said, Right, we're on easy meat here, they're bottom of the Second Division. Every team wanted to hammer the life out of us and it was like a Cup Final every game. It was marvellous. Well, it was marvellous for me. It wasn't too good for their nerves, but I thoroughly enjoyed it. In the six games I played we had an unbeaten run for four of them. It was great. It was only because of injuries at Tottenham that I went back. It was a complete surprise to me to go back at that time because it wasn't in my mind that I'd be going back at all, and I think

Bill Nicholson knew that. Once I'd left Tottenham on loan to Fulham, I felt that everybody—I really mean the club—had now come to the conclusion that I was no longer a First Division player. And I went back with the attitude of proving—as I'd had to do eight years before—that I was the best wing-half they had at that time. I had to go back and do the same thing again. So this is what geared me up most of all. I went back and played as well, I think, as I'd ever played for Tottenham Hotspur.

They wanted me to stay at Tottenham, but I'd now made up my mind that I'd proved all I had to prove at Tottenham. I didn't have to prove any more than I was a good player. By half-way through the short period I'd made up my mind that I had to start somewhere else, because I didn't want the problems of having any sort of injury and having to really hope and pray that I got back in the side. I didn't want the aggravation of that. I wanted to just go out and play.

I've enjoyed the football as much as I ever have. The only thing I do miss from the First Division is — not the Cup competitions or seeing it on television or things like that — but the atmosphere of the crowd. At Fulham, I think the most we've had is something like 18,000 or 20,000, against Aston Villa. It was very good that day, but on average our gates are about 10,000. Whereas at Tottenham the average was about 35,000 per home gate. This is the thing I miss most of all.

I think in the First Division you very very rarely see indifferent players. They're all of a high quality. Some are great players, some are good players and some are average players — but I think they're all *good* players in the First Division. I can't really say this in the Second Division. There's a lot of players playing in the Second Division who would really struggle in the First Division. No doubt about that. Burnley are doing well at the moment, they've got a fine side, a very good young side, but I think if they get to the First Division they're going to have problems.

I would think that most of the sides in the First Division are much fitter than the vast majority of the sides in the Second. I think what's helped teams like Norwich, they've been superbly trained throughout the summer. At Fulham we train extremely hard. I think we're probably one of the hardest-trained Second Division sides in the country. But I would think that half the Second Division sides don't train half as hard as we do. This is basically the difference between the two Leagues: the First Division is supremely fit.

I think you've got the pace and you've got the quality there in the Second Division. The only thing they don't do is that they don't perhaps think as quickly as in the First Division. It's the thinking which has helped me a lot, after playing eight or nine years at Tottenham. It gets you out of all sorts of trouble, whereas a lot of people in the Second Division don't think quickly enough really. This has been a big advantage. It's funny, I've now got the problem which I found when I came back from Mexico — the first game I'd encountered it — that people from the other sides started to mark me. They want to stop me playing. They stick somebody on me and say, Well, we won't give Mullery a kick today, we'll lose a man, but they'll lose Mullery as well. I never really got that a great deal in the First Division, except as I

Mullery with Fulham. "I'm so involved in the game, no different from the First Division. . . . I'm sure I train harder. . . . Everybody seems to look to me to play well. . . ."

say when I'd had a fairly good World Cup and I found players were picking me up for most games. But I find it quite regularly now in the Second Division.

We had a hell of a good run this last season. At one point, in 12 League games we were only beaten once. The nice thing about it is that you're winning and everybody's happy, but the day we lost against Cardiff, I was very disappointed—emotionally upset. I didn't really know what to say. It was as bad as any time in the First Division.

I've found I'm so involved in the game, no different from in the First Division. I've had my name taken and been involved in incidents. Actually I find more incidents in the Second Division involving me than I did in the First Division. People try and stop you playing and some people really go to extremes. If someone goes past me the old adrenalin gets up. I've got to get him, and get that ball back.

I certainly don't feel that I can take it all in my stride now, at 30. I feel I've got to train harder and got to work more than when I was a First Division player. If I don't then there's no doubt that I will go down and down and down, and be nothing but a failure. I'm sure I train harder now than I did when I was at Tottenham. There were so many good players in that side who would help you out at times—but now, it's funny, every time we go out on a Saturday everybody seems to look to me and if I don't play well, then the players in my side are very disappointed and they don't play well.

37

From Planned Goals to Trusting in Luck

TED MacDOUGALL's last season was the complete reverse of Alan Mullery's. While Mullery found security and satisfaction in his permanent move from Spurs in the First to Fulham in the Second, MacDougall found insecurity and disillusionment in his move from Bournemouth in the Third to Manchester United in the First. Such a leap was as dramatic as any there has been in a League transfer. MacDougall was thrown in at the deep end, and was in action immediately, playing alongside the most skilful players in the game, and against the best defences. And that was not all. As he says himself, the internal dramas which followed amounted to "one explosion after another". MacDougall talks here about the differences, and problems, he encountered in his new life at the top.

I expected to find a big difference, after all I'd read about it. You form your opinion from what you read and if you're not very careful you start believing that people are superhuman beings in the First Division. You know, they don't make mistakes. Well, it's just not true. I didn't really know if I could do it, when I came in, but I know now I can, if I get the service.

I've only been impressed with one or two teams. I was very impressed with Spurs. Not so much with Leeds, Liverpool, Arsenal. Spurs played ever so well. One-touch, two-touch football. It was simple. Not like Manchester United, where you've got to beat four or five players, like, and hit 30- or 40-yard passes before they'll believe you're

playing. Spurs don't play it like that at all. It's simple stuff. It looked great. But at Old Trafford the crowd's been brought up on players like Best and Moore and Charlton showing their skills.

I don't think the speed of the game was all that different. I didn't feel out of place, put it like that: I didn't feel a yard, two yards, slower than the rest. I think probably your speed of thought has got to be a bit quicker. You've got to have closer control, this kind of thing, but the actual speed of the game is not much different.

There's more individual skill sort of under the surface in the First, and what you find is that when teams get several goals up, then they take the mickey, like, they'll be out to show how much better than you they really are, they go and do their tricks, and that's when your skilful players come into it. But when you're in the Third Division and you're maybe three goals up you don't stop. You carry on. You try and get more goals, but you don't go out to humiliate the others.

At Bournemouth, when I was scoring well, it wasn't just an 'instinct' for goals — I had players around me who were prepared to give me the ball, when they saw that I was in a position to score. I think that's the biggest difference that I found in going to Manchester United. The players play for themselves a little bit more. You had to find your own opportunities. It was very difficult. You might think it ought to be the opposite way round, with all the planning and teamwork in the *First*. But a team like Bournemouth would go out every day practising for things and

when they happened on a Saturday, you knew exactly what was going to come off. You'd have half a yard start on the man marking you because you knew where the ball was going, and you'd only got to nick it and it was a goal. And they used to play to me a lot more, obviously, but at Manchester it was more luck than judgment really. Just luck being in the right spot at the right time really, because none of the goals were ever planned. I would say, 65 or 70 per cent of my goals at Bournemouth were planned, they were good goals because they were 'worked' goals, and it was two or three people knowing what each other was going to do with the ball. But, I'd say, *no* percentage at Manchester United, because you just didn't know what somebody else was

The MacDougall special of two seasons ago, for Bournemouth against Aston Villa. " . . . flying into that space knowing that the ball was coming in, I was there and the defender was behind me and, flick, it would be in."

going to do when they got the ball. That in itself is hard.

A typical goal for me at Bournemouth was the one against Villa, the diving header. That was typical of what happened because Tony Scott, a great little winger, he didn't used to beat anybody, he used to just get an angle on the full-back and knock it in to the near post and I used to be dragging the centre-half to the far post and leaving the space at the near post, and then come flying into that space knowing that the ball was coming in—I was there and the defender was behind me and, flick, it would be in. I used to get so many goals like that. They don't do it at Manchester. They've got to beat somebody. Well, the space has gone then. Defenders get back. They're good players at what they're doing, but they weren't doing it for me, they're doing it for themselves.

I'm not the kind of player that Manchester United may be used to—that can take on three or four players, waltz round them and then smash the ball. That's not my game. I need other

Ted MacDougall in Manchester United's colours. "You just didn't know what somebody else was going to do when they got the ball. That in itself was hard."

players to make them for me. I've found that I can score goals. I know I can score goals in the First Division. As I say, if I get the service. That's the most important thing.

One night I went to watch Bournemouth against Rochdale. There were three and a half thousand people there. I just couldn't see myself going back to that and playing in front of that kind of crowd. The crowd at Old Trafford were very good, I got letters when I was pulled off. Even though I wasn't playing well from the time I came—not as well as I knew I could play. I think it's a matter of feeling your way in, really. From the time I came from the Third Division, for four months it was sort of one big explosion after another. It started with Best, he left, then Frank O'Farrell went, then Docherty took over, then they bought all those new players. With Manchester United you're never really allowed to settle anyway. They're always in the public eye and they expect so much of players. It was very difficult, much more difficult than it would have been, say, with some other team that never gets half the publicity. It would have been nice and easy to settle in and play football. You're never really allowed to do that. The club's got this allure, I don't know what it is, but they get so much publicity, rightly or wrongly, and you're always in the limelight. But they also get the crowds. There's only one club in the country, really. I know that from my sports shop down in Bournemouth. It's all the Manchester United stuff that sells.

From the Land of the Long Ball to the Country of the Midfield

COLIN STEIN, previously the Glasgow Rangers and Scotland striker, came south last season, to Coventry in the English First Division. Stein's record in the Scottish League was 116 goals in 184 games (and his move from Hibernian to Rangers the first six-figure transfer in Scotland). Many Scottish players are signed as youths by English clubs, and this was an unusual move for a Scot of his age —25—and international standing. There was an uncertainty about Stein's current form, and there must have been a question mark as to whether the chemistry would work. Happily, it did. Stein talks here about his new niche and the difference between the English and Scottish game.

The differences are really from Hibernian to Rangers, and then from Rangers to Coventry. Hibs are one of the top clubs now in Scotland, but they were small then. There were only the two then—Rangers and Celtic—and as far as atmosphere especially goes there were only about four games a year. Six, maybe—including the derbies against Hearts. Then at Rangers the crowds were much bigger, much more atmosphere, tremendous pressure especially in the Rangers-Celtic matches, every game was a big occasion. But then we started going off, and the crowds dwindled to something like 10,000 or 15,000. And, you know, Ibrox holds over 100,000, so your 15,000 in fact looks like about 2,000. But down here in England, perhaps you don't get the crowds all that much bigger, but the grounds are smaller and they're full, and crowds are close around you and it seems to create a lot of atmosphere.

I had sort of lost my confidence with Rangers. But I've got it back and started playing well again. In the first few

Colin Stein in the Rangers' shirt (behind, Billy McNeill of Celtic). "I would rather be competitive all the way, that's the only way I can play."

weeks here the team weren't playing too well, but with Tommy Hutchison coming from Blackpool it all seemed to click. Everything seemed to fit into place. And I never had any trouble with the pace of it. You know, they say that Scottish football is slower than English football, but everything was going well, and it just seemed the same for pace.

What is different down here in Eng-

land is that there's a lot more playing back, playing backwards to go forwards. Backwards and across. Up in Scotland they used the long ball a lot, especially Rangers, for me to chase. The high, long ball, not just aimed at the target man but maybe at an open space for me to run into. They do it here too, sometimes—the striker has to be directly available to the fullback if the fullback's under pressure. But it doesn't happen that much here. They play a lot more football. Coventry do anyway. A good footballing side. This is the tactical outlook of it. You're told to try and play

FROM THE LAND OF THE LONG BALL
TO THE COUNTRY OF THE MIDFIELD

your way out of trouble instead of just kicking the ball up the park. At times, if you're under pressure, it becomes a bit difficult. But you try and play through the team, through the midfield.

Every game here there's a lot of pressure. There's no easy games. There's not a lot of difference between the top teams and bottom teams. But in Scotland you often went out against a team with your own personal attitude of 'Oh well, we'll beat these, they're maybe that yard slower . . .' Here you've got to be on your toes the whole time. I'd rather have it that way, than have easy games. I would rather be competitive all the way, because that's the only way I can play. Messing about and that, it doesn't suit my style.

Of course Rangers-Celtic matches were different. Yes, I enjoyed them. I didn't enjoy losing, but you have to play in those games to realise the tension and what it means to lose. But on the park it's fantastic, the crowd roaring and a tremendous noise from one end and a tremendous noise from the other. Fantastic. I suppose only the Cup Final here would equal it, or the England-Scotland international. The biggest atmosphere here so far was in two good derbies against Birmingham City and West Brom, one of them on Boxing Day. Two nil-all draws in fact. But they came here to defend, they didn't come to play.

I've been pleased with the crowd reaction. The Rangers fans are a lot harder to please, and if you haven't scored early, or don't look like scoring, they get on your back and start giving you the stick. Well, it was said they were the same down here, they say that Coventry supporters are hard to please, but I've never experienced it. They've been great. We've been winning, of course. Sixteen points out of 18 at one time.

This business of tackling from behind, that they tightened up on two seasons ago, they still do it in Scotland but not to the same extent as down here. I used to watch the English games on television and some of them were terrible. No intention of playing the ball, just going right through. You know, really going in to hurt somebody.

They do more on the ball in Scotland, there're a lot more individuals. They want to show their skills. You've got a lot of twopenny-halfpenny ball players that can kick the ball and that, but they can't run. There's a lot of them. But don't get me wrong, there're a lot of good players too.

There are good players in England too, who can play a bit. But not so much as individuals—more within the team. The teamwork is much better down here tactically. If they're told to do things they do them. There's not much room for the Jimmy Johnstones, and that, in English football. Because you get found out, how you play, and you soon get snuffed out.

There's not much that the English game lacks really. You've got everything down here. It's a footballer's paradise, isn't it? You know, anybody good can make it to the top. The rewards now for a First Division player are fantastic.

From Working until Saturday to Working for Saturday

For many, life in the Fourth Division is a struggle. For some, it is dismal. But for Hereford United, giant killers in the Cup two seasons ago, admitted to the League last season, life in the Fourth Division has been dynamic.

Their gates averaged around 8,000, about 3,000 up on any other club in the Fourth. Like professionals at the top of the First, they met for a hotel lunch before each home game. After a sticky start, they put together four wins in a row and moved up eight places, and were soon heading for the top of the ladder. This, despite the fact that player-manager Colin Addison broke his leg in the first away match. "When I broke my leg," he was able to joke, "I think I strengthened the side." Certainly he was able to give more time to management and coaching. A First Division footballer with Notts Forest and Arsenal, Addison's last experience of the *Fourth* Division was 15 years previously, with York. He found the Fourth more competitive than when he last knew it, and certainly a hard Division. Everyone found it different, in varying degrees, from the Southern League. Some others, like Addison, were re-adjusting to a game in which they had had some prior experience.

Some of the amateurs went on with their week-day jobs — like Roger Griffiths, who works in a Hereford canning factory, and Brian Owen, an electricity salesman in Winsley, some sixty-five miles away on the Somerset-Wiltshire border. Especially for Owen, 29, life has not been very much different, though the football has been. The game was quicker and harder and more competitive and, as a striker, he found he needed to be much sharper in taking his chances; but he tuned in. Otherwise, out of the way of supporters and local press, his working week was much as it was, and disappointments on the Saturday were soon swallowed. The change of life with Division football, the new pressures both on and off the pitch, have made a much greater impact on a player like BILLY TUCKER, a 24-year-old centre-half. Tucker was an amateur first with Evesham and then Hereford, and before last season was employed as an accountant.

★　　★　　★

1972. Cup defeat for Newcastle. Inset: Colin Addison.

It's been a new experience, alright. Compared with the Southern League it's more physical, and the players are fitter. Half way through the first match I was shattered. In amateur football you might get one or two shirkers in any team, but not among pros. All the players are good players, the competition's more fierce and consequently there's more work to do. I'm now pushing up for corners and set-piece situations, much more involved in everything that's happening on the field.

Personally, I *enjoy* the games just as much as I enjoyed them as an amateur, but you're also much more aware of the pressure. You're thinking about Saturday's game all week, working for it, and if you lose it's a week's work down the drain. It's much worse when you lose, as a pro. You have to live with it. It stays with you. And, whereas you usually get Monday off if you win, as a sort of bonus, if you lose and perhaps haven't played too well you'll have to come in on the Monday. So you're well aware of losing. In Southern League days, if you lost you could still smile about it; and people would soon forget about the result.

45

I really do think the whole difference boils down to the pressure. There's no outlet. If you live in Hereford, everyone's talking about the last game. If you go out in the evening to have a drink or eat, people will recognise you and come up to talk about the last game. You're always reminded how important each result is to these people. I would compare it with Manchester, the way the results mean so much to the town. Everyone here knows Hereford United and are interested in us. They'll stop you in the street. It might be a novelty, but I think it's here to stay. If a player comes from another Fourth Division club he feels part of it here, he's known and respected.

We've been getting these bigger gates, and the crowd's been responding and we've responded to them. When we were drawing 0-0 against Bradford, they started roaring us on. Most of the lads think the crowd gave us our victory that day. Really, these supporters deserve something a lot better than a Fourth Division club. It's not really a Fourth Division club anyway, the way the players and supporters are treated. Our supporters deserve higher division football, and one day they'll have it, when we get promotion.

[Hereford subsequently finished second and won promotion.]

Death
of a Team

Barrow always did seem to have the odds against them. Far out on a limb of the North-West — like Workington above them — their away travelling was amongst the longest and most arduous in all the Football League. They found few players from their own area and were forced to rely on cheaply-priced players from afar, many in the last stage of their careers. Barrow, for all its many years in the League, could boast few distinctions. Its Cup run never went beyond the third round. Previous to its elimination from the League, the players who had gone on from Barrow to better, or other, clubs numbered only five. The 'highest-ranked' of these has been George Smith of Birmingham City. (The others are Tony Field of Blackburn, Keith Eddy of Watford, Tony Morrin of Exeter, and David Workington of Grimsby.) In circulation now are another five players. This is what has happened to them, and the rest of their teammates.

Striker **John Rowlands**, formerly with Stockport, was sold to Workington for £1,200 — the top price among the five. His new manager, George Aitken, has found him good value — "strong in the air, and agile for a big lad, he causes trouble for defenders in the Fourth Division and he makes chances for other people around him."

Mick Hollis, whom Barrow had just moved from defence to attack, has been a success in that role for Chester, who bought him for £1,000. He promises to prove the best of the Barrow Bargains. "He's certainly done a good job for me," says Chester manager Ken Roberts, "playing as striker, and getting

goals. He could go high in the game, he's only 22 now, but this is something you just don't know."

Bobby Noble, originally from Newcastle, was sold to Colchester after a month's trial, for £1,000. An orthodox

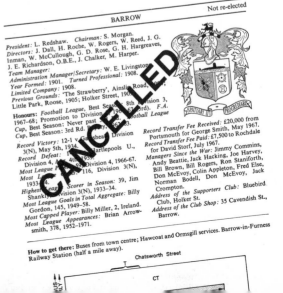

Not re-elected

BARROW

President: L. Redshaw. Chairman: S. Morgan.
Directors: J. Dall, H. Roche, W. Rogers, W. Reed, J. G. Inman, W. McCullough, G. D. Rose, G. H. Hargreaves, J. E. Richardson, O.B.E., J. Chalker, M. Harper.
Team Manager:
Administration Manager/Secretary: W. E. Livingstone
Year Formed: 1901. Turned Professional: 1908.
Limited Company: 1908.
Previous Grounds: 'The Strawberry', Ainslie Road,
Little Park, Roose, 1905; Holker Street, 190
Honours: Football League, Best Sea   8th   ision 3,
1967–68; Promotion to Division   196   67   rd). F.A.
Cup, Best Season: Never past   otball League
Cup, Best Season: 3rd Rd.   62   3.
Record Victory: 12-1 v Ga shea   Division
3(N), May 5th, 1934.
Record Defeat: artlepools U.,
Division 4,   4th   Division 4, 1966-67.
Most League   116, Division 3(N),
1933   4.
Highest eagu Scorer in Season: 39, Jim
Shankl   vision 3(N), 1933–34.
Most League Goals in Total Aggregate: Billy
Gordon, 145, 1949–58.
Most Capped Player: Billy Miller, 2, Ireland.
Most League Appearances: Brian Arrow-smith, 378, 1952–1971.

Record Transfer Fee Received: £20,000 from
Portsmouth for George Smith, May 1967.
Record Transfer Fee Paid: £7,500 to Rochdale
for David Storf, July 1967.
Managers Since the War: Jimmy Commins,
Andy Beattie, Jack Hacking, Joe Harvey,
Bill Brown, Bill Rogers, Ron Staniforth,
Don McEvoy, Colin Appleton, Fred Else,
Norman Bodell, Don McEvoy, Jack
Crompton.
Address of the Supporters Club: Bluebird
Club, Holker St.
Address of the Club Shop: 35 Cavendish St.,
Barrow.

CANCELLED

How to get there: Buses from town centre; Hawcoat and Ormsgill services. Barrow-in-Furness Railway Station (half a mile away).

Chatsworth Street

CT

'big centre-half' with Barrow, he has been used by Colchester elsewhere in the back four, especially as a 'sweeper'. But Colchester are not sure if he figures in their long-term planning, and will "probably let him go".

Eddie Garbett, a lively winger, and **Malcolm Russell**, a solid midfield player, were both bought by Stockport for £1,000 each. The manager who bought them was Brian Doyle, who was previously with nearby Workington. "The two boys have done well for me," says Doyle. "Garbett's a quick little fellow and he's got a terrific shot — it's over 70 mph, almost in the Lee and Lorimer class. He could certainly go further in the game. Russell's a good pro, he knows the game well, he likes to win and he's a leader. He also scored two very valuable goals, from midfield, in the Cup — one against Bradford City, and the other the first goal of the match against West Ham.

"In fact I thought Barrow was unlucky to go out, I felt they weren't so bad a side at all. Actually I went after the whole five of those players. I thought it was a bargain whoever you got at that price. They were valued at about £5,000 each."

In fact the value which the League had put on the five, in controlling the selling, was £28,000. Barrow received £5,200. Russell, sold for £1,000, had cost Barrow £6,500 just one year previously.

Other contracts had the second of two years still to run and were honoured. These players continued to play for Barrow in the Northern Premier League. Some at first decided to stay, and then moved elsewhere — one to Skelmersdale United, also in the Northern Premier League, another to Everton as Youth Coach. One of the best remaining prospects is a local boy — one of the few the League team had known — **Ian McDonald**, who is keen to move on into the Football League, and likely to. Some other players had been released for disciplinary reasons, one after a court case concerning the 'theft' of a football. Others, already given free transfers, are now out of football — gone back to betting shops in Wakefield or the building trade in Carlisle . . .

Don McEvoy, manager in the last three years, is now a publican in Brighouse, Yorkshire. "The downfall of Barrow was due to a lot of things," he says. "A lot of mistakes were made. Players were brought in, never drawn from the Barrow area. And players brought who hadn't proved themselves, and they didn't prove themselves for Barrow either. The management and the players were against each other at the end. Really and truly we forgot the most important thing, which was football itself."

Only one man, though, has really gone down with Barrow. The club was a life's work for its secretary, Wilf Livingstone, and in his office was a model of his ultimate dream — a new, £30,000 grandstand. After 12 years, Wilf Livingstone has gone back to the firm that nearly everyone in Barrow works for, back to a job in the drawing office at Vickers.

Decisive action in Tottenham goal area, as Jennings punches out, high above Holland and Robson of West Ham.

CWF

Day of the Scout

Ten games a week. Forty thousand miles a year. All in search of the youngsters who can "really dig it in", in hitting a ball, who can "spray it around": the young soccer stars of tomorrow who will continue the glory of the Gunners.

Ernie Collett of Arsenal starts this bleak Saturday at Highbury at 9.30 a.m., checks his mail, and sets off to watch Newham v. South London in Plaistow, E.13 — an under-15 English schools FA trophy competition. He's checking on certain reports he's received about a couple of "promising lads".

Gordon Clark and Ernie Collett, two full-time Arsenal scouts, spend their days vetting the reports that pour in from the thirty scouts who are scattered around the British Isles, a web to catch the young soccer star. At the age of 16 a boy can be signed as an apprentice footballer and in a competitive, expensive world that signature can be worth literally hundreds of thousands of pounds. Yet Ernie Collett is adamant: "We want players for Arsenal. We're not interested in their cash value."

In the afternoon, with Ernie Collett off in Chelmsford, Gordon Clark, Arsenal's chief scout, watches the youngsters who *have* made it. These are the six or seven a year who sign as apprentices and now wear the crisp red-and-white of Arsenal. Sitting in the Directors' box, he's watching a Football Combination match against Chelsea. Amongst the Arsenal players are Marinello, Barnett and Nelson; in Chelsea's side, Baldwin, playing with a marked lack of interest.

What is Clark looking for? "Their progress, basically. We've got two players down on loan from Sunderland, and then there's our own youngsters. There's young Powling. He's only 16, but you watch him. He's a leader, a born captain."

What happens if they fail to make the grade? "We give them a year or two to settle in. But if they're not making the progress we expect we call the parents and explain the position and then help the lad with any further plans."

Gordon Clark develops the same point as Ernie Collett — the care that Arsenal give to the young apprentice. "The governor insists upon it." It's clear that Bertie Mee's presence is clearly and widely felt and respected.

What are his general duties as a chief

scout? "Organising the scouts around the country. Checking on the reports that they send each week. Each scout covers two or three games a week. When I receive a particularly good series of reports on a player then I must go and see him. I was in Arbroath on Thursday. Tomorrow I'm off to Cork."

It's a long way to go: he must feel very certain that there's a good player over there. "No, I'm just going to confirm my doubts. This particular lad is 20 and no one who's good is going to escape that long. If they're going to make it, they've been signed long before that."

Gordon points out two of the players who are now playing in a virtually empty stadium at Highbury. "Look at *him*. Bags of confidence. But he'll never make it. Good on the left foot but his right's a swinger. Once that gets around, the defenders will just sit on his left side, and he's had it. And that one over there, only 16, promising, but what I call a stutterer. He's not playing instinctively. He's hesitating too much. I think perhaps he's outgrown his strength for a while. Perhaps if we can give him some time he'll fill out and come through." The boy in question is a tall beanpole. The truth of Gordon's comment becomes evident. The boy seems unsure of his next move and often seems to be in the way rather than helping.

What about goalkeepers? "They're difficult," he says. He goes on to talk of the top goalkeepers in the country, and how Arsenal are interested in one

of them, particularly—"but you watch him, when he dives his backside hits the ground first. It should be the shoulders first."

How many boys actually make it? "A few only. You know, there's not many schoolboy internationals that make it. It's often the youngsters who come through in stages, mature slowly." And many players, he says emphatically, are spoilt. "I'd like to fine them for not trying sometimes, but the governor won't have it." Gordon Clark is very keen on discipline and the boys' character on the field. "They've got to think, think, think all the time. Look at them now. Draw a circle of 40 yards diameter and you've got all 20 players there. They're not stretching the game. You *must* use the park." Gordon Clark expects, and demands, concentration.

How would he sum up the indications of a good player, then? "Ability, determination, all-out effort." He considers it, and adds: "The lads from the north are harder. They've got more grit." He punches out this comment as the game ends and he turns to go down to the dressing rooms. There he bandies a few jokes and raw humour and then he's off.

What's on next week? It's almost an irrelevant question. "Could be anywhere. Cork on Sunday, and then anywhere there's a game of football and a promising youngster."

So *you* want to be a professional footballer? What do you need? Well, you need to be a schoolboy star. You need to be a one in a million player for Ernie and Gordon and Arsenal.

Anguish from Charlie George as an Arsenal shot goes wide. McCormick of Crystal Palace seems to see it differently.

Keith Weller, clearing for Leicester against Ipswich.

I'm Sorry Ref, I Let you Down

ROGER KIRKPATRICK is the referee who entertains. His expressive flourishes also seem to charm the players and to keep the game flowing. His appearance at a game is said to add some 3,000 on a Division gate, and his 'local' club, Nuneaton, used to guarantee to break the ground record when he went there. A 40-year-old sales director with a hosiery firm, the referee's kit which he wears, and markets, is of his own design. He is known as 'The man who introduced the handkerchief'—the white top pocket—and his newest kit features shirt and shorts in an all-in-one suit. The referee who has brought fashion and entertainment into the game talks here about discipline-with-pleasure, and about the photos on these pages (Spurs v. West Bromwich and, over page, Everton v. Manchester United).

The only way is to try and enjoy the game. I'm sure if everybody enjoyed it and played it, I won't say for the love of it, but played it for the enjoyment of it, it would be a much better game. There's nothing wrong with it now, basically. That's all it's about, two lots of fellows kicking that little ball about and trying to get it into the net, but it's not life and death.

There has been criticism made against me, people have said they go to see the game and not me. At times people in the press have had a go at me. But this game is called football and it's supposed to be an entertainment as well. I don't go there with any specific ideas to entertain. But I was born a Leo and I understand all Leos are extroverts, so I'm afraid my father will have to take the blame for that. I don't do it with any pre-set ideas. It is me, purely my character, and I'm not going to change. On the other hand, people have learnt to live with me as much as I've learnt to live with them and they've accepted me as part of the game. And I know there are people who want to know where I'm refereeing and who'll follow me to that game.

There's no particular formula for dealing with trouble. I feel that one's got to have a basic sense of man-management and psychology. I never make a player come to me. I always *request* him, and he always does. I put the onus on the player. I deal with 'situations' as fairly as possible and

I like to be seen to be fair. Again, it comes back to man-management and getting the respect of the players. There are certain players that I never have any trouble with at all, and others from whom I just don't seem to get the same sort of reaction. It's just human nature. There are some people you can get on with and some you can't. I try desperately to be seen to be fair at all times.

I remember one player, I was about to send him off, and he was apologising. He was apologising for letting *me* down as a referee. And I was sending him off. And he felt he'd let me down. We were quite close friends before and we still are now, and that was two or three seasons ago.

"Alistair Brown of West Brom just about to kick the ball away after a free kick has been given — I know Alistair quite well as an ex-Leicester City player — and I was saying, 'Ah-ah, Alistair.'"

I'M SORRY REF, I LET YOU DOWN

Decisions imminent? Above: the referee watches from a distance as possession is contested by the hand of Chelsea keeper Phillips and the foot of Alan Ball for Arsenal. Left: O'Hare of Derby moves for goal, between Hinton (left) and Dempsey of Chelsea.

"That was for an indirect free kick to be taken from the spot I'm pointing at. It was for a very high tackle by Mike England on Bobby Gould."

I'M SORRY REF, I LET YOU DOWN

As for swearing, I must be honest. Nobody swears directly at me under any circumstances. I'm a great believer in this and the players know it. On the other hand, if a player does a wild pass or something and he turns round and lets a mouthful go and he's in my ear-shot they just look at me, and I say 'Crumbs, I've got to go to Church twice tomorrow to forgive my sins as well as yours.' This sort of kills it. You can't book every player that swears on the field. However, if it's directly at me there's only one option. They'll go, with me, and I think they know it.

You may say that giving a penalty always causes dissent, but I must be honest and say I'd given about eight by mid-season and had no bother whatsoever. I'm touching wood now with both hands, but when I've given a

With Bernard of Everton. "He was saying, as far as I can recall, 'Stop running past me so fast, it makes me look as if I've not done any training.' I told him he wasn't as old as all that."

With George Best. "That's Best getting a right rapping. I'm just watching to see what's happening before turning around to Best. He met my disfavour by making a remark off the ball, probably characteristic of him, but not of the game. It was knocking the game."

penalty I've not had players gathered round me. I will not have them. Again, I think your reputation goes ahead of you.

Take that photograph of John Fitzpatrick's name being taken. John wasn't arguing. In fact what John was saying to me when he was being booked was: 'Oh God, I've been off 11 months. In my first game back I get booked.' He's not questioning the right. As you see, we've both got our heads down looking at the book, but as I said to him: 'I didn't do the thing, I'm only carrying out what the statutory laws require me to do. If you break the law, I'll take the necessary action.' But John's not complaining. In fact, it was most unfortunate for the boy because he had a great match. But he did a very high and late tackle.

If a man's at all sensitive, things said

With Fitzpatrick of Manchester United. "It was most unfortunate for the boy because he had a great match. But he did a very high and late tackle."

against him must hurt. I'm very sensitive. Certain things have been said on the football field, and on the terraces. If I see them in the press it hurts, if I hear them it hurts. We're only out there to do our best for the game basically. It's a game we love and that's the end of it. It's the greatest game on God's earth as far as I'm concerned and involvement in it is a blessing. I'll crack a joke with the players and they'll crack one back.

You'd be surprised with the stories that get told during games! And the one-line gags. Mike Summerbee and Chris Simpkin, when Chris was playing for Hull City against Manchester City in the third round of the FA Cup, they got rather close together and I blew my whistle. Before I had time to say anything Mike Summerbee turns round and says to me, 'Sorry, Rog, we've got the handbags tangled up.' These are the sort of things that come out. I get a lot of cracks made at me from being in the hosiery trade. Have you fitted any good stockings lately? What's the price of your tights? There was a bomb scare once at Manchester City, and an announcement was made to the crowd. Mike Summerbee pointed at the ball and said, 'Check it to see if it's in that bloody thing.' I picked it up and shook it and put it to my ear, and that made the crowd laugh.

There are plenty of quips on the pitch. Quite a lot of them you can't repeat. There are times when even a short story comes out! They take the mickey out of the opposing side, or out of you, and it's all in good humour.

No Decision

No decision? Radford for Arsenal contests a high ball with Liverpool's Lloyd and Keegan (No. 7).

*No decision? Dougan for Wolves in contention
with Manchester City keeper Healey.*

That Bridgwater Crowd

What is it that makes a man, or a woman, support a far-distant football team? The most supported club in the country is Manchester United. Week after week, spectators there are surprised to hear a fellow supporter speaking with the strange, far-off accent of London, or Somerset, or North Wales . . . The visitors are regarded with curiosity. Why *do* they come and support United?

"Because I picked them out of a hat," is the usual answer of John Pitts, a 31-year-old sales rep from St Mary's Cray, Orpington, Kent. He says it started for him in '51, when he was 10 years old. At that time he didn't support any particular side, but he wanted to. He looked down the final League table, decided it was too easy to support the team who had won the League, and thought the side in fourth place seemed a good proposition. That side was Manchester United. John Pitts knew nothing of their history at all— not even their Cup win three years before. Now, Pitts is Secretary of the London and District Manchester United Supporters Club. It covers the southern half of England, and became, with the lapsing of the Supporters Club in Manchester, *the* Manchester United Supporters Club. "It was pure chance that I chose a club with a manager who chose players with skill and flair and great expression of the greatest

game in the world." Other people have a different story to tell, like "the Bridgwater crowd". Forty-five of them travel by coach, the 210 miles from West Somerset to Manchester, for each of United's home games. One night last season, gathered in the Blake Arms, Bridgwater, they testified their loyalty to Old Trafford.

"It started when I was twelve," says a lovely young lady named Margaret, from Bristol. "I followed them because of Bobby Charlton, I think." Margaret used to travel up on her own, and went in the Stretford End. She travelled by rail, starting from Bristol at 6 o'clock and getting back after midnight. The journey cost £5 then. A local newspaper story was written about her, followed later by a TV interview. She is the club's "TV star". This was how the club heard about her, and they now pick her up at Bristol every trip. Margaret has never watched Bristol City or Bristol Rovers. "There's no atmosphere.

And not people like this."

"Because of their attractive style of football," says John Steel. A Londoner, originally a West Ham supporter, he began following United when he was moved to Manchester. Then his company transferred him to its Bridgwater branch. He was delighted to find a Supporters Club there. "The thing about Old Trafford is the *club*. The supporters are so knowledgeable and appreciative of good football. The difference between Old Trafford and anywhere else is very hard to put your finger on. The difference is just the club, that's all I can say."

"I've always been a Manchester United man," says Mr L. C. Curtis. "When I was younger I went to watch Bristol City, but the class of football deteriorated. And the only other teams are Torquay, Exeter, and so forth." He used to live in Wells, and when he went back to Bridgwater he saw the club's advertisement in the paper. Many like him have joined through the ad.

"I followed Villa right through the War," says Mrs Doreen Read, apologetically, to a background of stormy complaint. "From the time of the Munich disaster I followed United. I came in right at the start of the club with my son. He's never been interested in anyone else."

"I'm a Mancunian," says the Chairman, Ted Hutchinson. "My father took me to Old Trafford when I was very small. I went to the other team, or our own, every week. My sister still sends me anything interesting from the Football Pink. I knew Ken Gurd went up regularly to Manchester, and we got together. It was his brainchild really."

"At school I played soccer," says Ken Gurd, the Secretary. "But you see this is a Rugby town. I used to follow Rugby and make trips up to Twickenham, and that. My lad took up soccer and I became interested again. I suppose I began to follow United because of

The George Best goal against Sheffield United . . . The shouting after it . . . When they scored a second, everyone was still talking about the first."

Denis Law (versus Blockley of Arsenal): nostalgia for the moments he made his own.

Munich, and because they are such a good team. There's no-one around here, so you look around the rest of the country and you pick the best." He claims there's no club in the country that treats its supporters like Manchester United does. When the Supporters Club tries to get tickets for United's away games the big London clubs, especially, "won't entertain you in your request". They couldn't get a block booking at Crystal Palace. But the Midland clubs are better.

"My love goes back," says a man called Stan, "to when they played Real Madrid a year or so before the disaster. I travelled up from Gibraltar. I always said then that I wanted to go and see United play on their own ground."

"My mates drifted off supporting teams like Arsenal and Leeds and Man-

chester City," says Eugene McCann, 16. "I went to Old Trafford on the coach one day, and the thing I remember is Denis Law scoring from 20 yards. He just turned and banged it in. And the atmosphere there—it sort of vibrates around you, the crowd's very close in."

Someone else remembers when they beat Spurs 2-1 in 1970, "and Bobby Charlton scored from a free kick, and hit another on the run".

"The George Best goal against Sheffield," says another. "The shouting after that. When Gowling scored a second goal there was hardly anything, because everyone was still talking about Best's."

"When Best went down on his knees," says Margaret. "When he scored in the Cup. I could have cried."

Another man remembers a header by Law, pushed over the bar by the full-back. "An emotional moment, that. A great goal just wiped away like that. And when you knew it was probably Law's last season . . ."

Will support for United fall away now with less success, and a new team?

"Where are the falling gates then?" they demand.

"You read Malcolm Allison saying that no red scarves are to be seen in Manchester. He must be colour blind."

"*No*, United won't lose any support with Scotsmen. We can't get enough Scots."

"It's not a disappointment if they change players. It wouldn't matter if they played an entirely new team." This statement is cheered.

"We like seeing new players and seeing how they play."

"We have faith that the club is trying to provide an entertainment day in and day out."

Their job, they emphasise, is to *sup-port*—not to offer advice or judgement. The Chairman quotes, as *their* policy also, a statement from a United programme at the time of the Crisis:

"We shall continue to support United, no matter who runs the club, who manages the team, and no matter who plays in the team . . ."

"Or which division we're in," adds a lady, to laughter.

They say that when they watch a game they don't shout very loudly and very rarely criticise. They tell of the amazement from people in the crowd around them. "A coach from Somer-

set! They think we are a bit soft in the head. One dreadful winter's day, a lady said to me: We're mad aren't we? We've come fourteen miles. I said, *We've* come 210 miles! She said, You're mad."

"Sometimes you only have to open your mouth, like in asking where a seat number is, and someone over-hears you and says: 'Oh, that's that Bridgwater crowd.'"

They describe how their driver, Bill —who has missed only two home games in four seasons—is so much King of the Road that people can set their watches at the 'checkpoints' on the four-hour journey. People who pass them on the motorway know who they are. They play Bingo twice up and once back. They don't talk a lot about the game—"Wasn't a bad game . . . so-and-so should have scored . . ." And that's it. They then listen to the radio for the other results. "And to hear which games had the biggest crowds. To see if we're in the top three again. You can guarantee it."

The Secretary of the Bridgwater branch of the Manchester United Sup-porters Club sent off a letter after the meeting in the Blake Arms. It ended thus:

. . . As this . . . . . . .ed at . . .ly morning return from Old Trafford . . . .ers, the number present, did no doubt convey to you the interest shown in United. I sincerely hope you thought your journey worthwhile. I can be quoted, if you like, as saying that I, Live, eat and sleep Man United. Many Thanks, Yours Sincerely, K. Gurd.

The Style
is the Man

On these pages, pictures of four Tottenham players—at least, four *heads*, and four *figures*, of Spurs players. Is each of them one and the same person? Which is, and which isn't?★ The clues lie in the physical style of each player. On the following pages, well-known individuals are once again portrayed by their style alone, and described in words by artist **PAUL TREVILLION**.

★Answers to these 'combinations', and the in-dividuals which follow, on page 93.

THE DANCER

He turns the football pitch into his stage. He doesn't run, he dances. He doesn't jump, he bounces. He does kick turns and high kicks, he skips about. Watch his light steps. It's almost as if he's moved by the music of the movement. And listen to the crowd. They make a different noise. Instead of the usual sort of deep-throated roar, when this fellow gets the ball there's a great mix of noises—there's a sigh, there are one or two girls screaming. It's the pop star sound. You don't get it with other players. Best had it and now this fellow's got it.

The other great thing about him is that he has what you can call the Denis Law quality. You don't see him. It's almost as if he's on stage, but in the dark—and then the spotlight picks him out and there he is. Turning it on.

And although he's a bouncy, cuddly little fellow, he's got this tremendous secret determination. His heading is sensational. He climbs high, very high, and he's rather like a toothpaste tube with the top taken off. You get two defenders, and the harder they squeeze him the higher he shoots. You're not going to keep him down.

He looks even smaller and cuddlier than he is because he's in a team of a lot of six-footers. You can see him standing next to some of these big, raw-boned fellows and you think, What a nice little lad. Well, he's not

physical, but he's hard. It's determination. He's a bundle of dynamite. He looks like he's pepped up. He looks like he's on cloud nine. He's the Teenybopper. The Music Man. The Dancer.

THE GUNFIGHTER

He's not a hero. Goalscorers are generally loved by kids. A Ted Mac-Dougall is the schoolboy hero, but not this fellow. He's got this enormous jaw like Desperate Dan. He's got these big long sideburns, like the old Westerners had. His hair looks as if it's been chiselled on his head. His head just seems to drop into his shoulders. And a tremendous chest. A tough, tough man. A throw-back to the heroes of the Wild West. This is the Gunfighter.

He's got bow legs. It looks as if he should be riding a horse. They say that: "Where's your horse?" At Tottenham once, Perryman got hurt and hit the ground. It was near the touchline. And this fellow walked over with that horse-rider's walk and he put his arm under him and he lifted him, and you could see suddenly it wasn't Perryman any more. It was one of those big saddles you see humped up by cowboys. That's what he did. He lifted him up, just as though he was a saddle with all the trappings and threw him over the touchline.

Watch him go through the middle, when the chance is on. There are two defenders and he hits them. He goes straight through them, straight between them. You see them bounce back, like swing doors. He's into the saloon, and it's one against one. Nobody else matters. He says so him-self. He looks at the goalkeeper as soon as he comes out: it's him and the goalkeeper. These two guys are meant to meet up.

You see the goalkeeper coming out and you say, He's got no chance. And he hasn't. The ball hits the back of the net like a body dropping. Bang. Then he looks at that left foot of his. You'd think he was going to bend down and blow the gunsmoke away.

THE CHARGER

This man is no footballer, he's an athlete. He runs with his chest sticking out. He looks like an athlete in a burst at the tape, thrusting himself forward. He runs in straight lines, and very very fast. It's a very exciting moment when he suddenly bursts out of the blocks. When the move breaks down, or he's off-side, it's as if he's been called back for a false start. It's a sad moment.

Also, when he's really moving, if he's done a hundred yards half of it's been made in the air. He's a triple jumper, he's a hop, skip and a jump champion, because when he goes past the first man, there's a little hop, he skips past the second and then there's the jump over the third, and then they hit him. They deck him and he hits the ground, like landing in the sand.

He's very top heavy, and when he's tackled he goes down forwards, on his chest. The whole of the front of his chest picks up everything, a red badge of blood, and the black mud of the park. It looks as if he's wearing a different coloured strip. He's also one of football's gentlemen. He's the first to go and pick a player up if he falls down. He'll retrieve the ball for the opposition. He's very apologetic. Everything about his play is apologetic.

He's got everything, except the devil. When he was with his former club, he looked a world-class player — if only he had good people to play with.

But maybe he learnt to do it on his own. Maybe he can't use good players. His great strength remains in those lonely, electric runs.

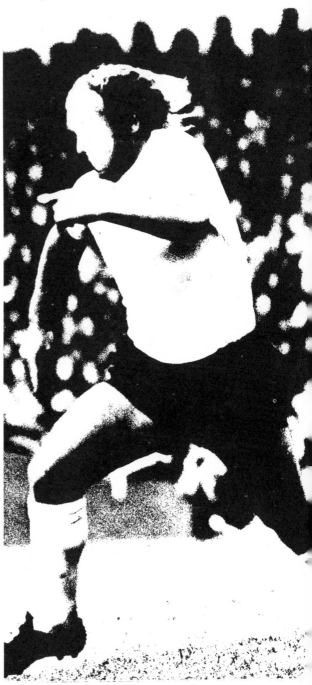

PINGER

He's rated to have one of the hardest shots in football. He's scored a lot of goals from outside the box, and he takes all the free kicks from outside the box. He's got a tremendously powerful right-foot shot, but the secret of his striking of the ball is that he *pings* it and they're stingers. They ping and they sing and they sting.

And he's never better than when he's in a fight. He's a real fighter. He's always going forward, and if the team's three up he plays as if he's on the other side and they're three down. He's a great man for lost causes. In other words, he'll chase a ball down which looks like it's going out of play. He's the fellow that never says it's out. Every ball to him, if it's in his area, is worth chasing down.

And he'll get the balls he's no right to. Not only does he get them but he gets them back across the park. And they've scored from this sort of situation. He's the sort of fellow if ever he was running for a bus and he missed it at one stop, he'd chase it to the next stop. He's going to catch it. He'll hunt that bus down.

When he finishes a game, somebody said, his shoes carry on running for 20 minutes after he's taken them off. That's some player. He never seems battle-worn—which is a bit of a cheat, because his team plays in a dark strip and the scars of battle don't show. He looks as fresh as paint. He's little and he's got a high-pitched voice that can be heard squeaking out. It's wrong to think that this fellow is just a worker. He's got all the skills. But he excels in the unglamorous parts of the game.

THE DENTIST

He's the man they call Tarzan. They call him Tarzan because he's got absolutely no shoulders at all. They reckon that he always has to wear a tie, that if he undoes the top button his shirt automatically falls down. He looks very hunched, he looks like a dentist, in white, as he waits there for forwards to come at him. And just like when you go to the dentist — when you get there the pain suddenly goes away, you don't want to be there — so it is with the forwards. They no longer want to go around him, so they take the easy way out. They just disappear, they pass the ball somewhere else. They pass the buck. When he senses he's in trouble, the first thing he does after a heavy tackle, a real banger, is to raise his right hand to the referee; like a policeman on point duty. He always does it, raises the right hand. Now if the ref continues to come, he then throws in the smile, the big Burt Lancaster type of smile, and the little wave of the hand. If that fails and the referee still walks, he uses his right hand and puts it on the referee's shoulder, bends his head, smiles the huge smile and he does the persuasive talk. If all that ends, the hand comes down, slaps his thigh, he turns and walks off. He's been booked.

He's got the most educated left foot in the business. They call it the Extractor, the Pincer. That's the thing which removes the ball. With this left foot of his he can do anything. He could unscrew a bottle top with it. People have said that he's only got one foot. In fact, he's probably got one of the best *right* foots in the team, but he's never given credit for it. He never has to use it.

THE WINDMILL

Some unkind things have been said about this footballer. It's been said that he couldn't trap a medicine ball. And that when he backheels the ball it finishes in front of him. He is very awkward. In fact, he's got all the talents—but somebody's got in there with an egg-whisk and mixed them all up. He's liable to do anything. One minute he'll trip over a ball and the next he'll beat somebody on a six-pence. He runs stiffly, but with a long stride, and a lot quicker than he appears to.

In the air he's tremendous. It's the old old saying, he times his jump better than the others and he gets up there. But this fellow, when he heads a ball, he can be nodding to somebody about 40 blocks away because he hits it with power. He's got so much power, when he heads the ball the people behind the goal duck.

With his great strength and his awkwardness he's a great target man. He's easily seen on the park. He's got both legs and both arms going at the same time. You can pick him up, you can bang him with the ball. But, surprisingly, awkward as he is, he has got an ability that all great players have, in that he can hide in exposed places.

He's bony and hard, cold and craggy, like a bit of Scottish rock. He's like a sword. You don't know which side of him is sharp, or whether it's going to be sharp or blunt, and sometimes he's very deceiving. And he's like a windmill, because everything's moving on him, his legs, his arms. He is awkward and he does use his arms to balance himself. He sticks them right out, bent from the elbow. Like the windmill, he's always going.

The Best Cup Final Goals

In past years, this book has featured the Cup Final goals, with sequences taken from newsreel film.★ The best of these, with a new goal added, are collected here. Each of these are outstanding goals, involving individual skill, and at least one may be called a great goal. They were all scored by the winning side, and each was the winning, or decisive, goal. The four goals are discussed by MALCOLM ALLISON.

The Manchester City goal is really Summerbee's. He had been giving young David Nish a pasting, and had already got to that position on the line two or three times. He went down again and beat his man, went around the outside of him, looked to see where the other players were, and absolutely played the ball back into that space. He put five defenders and the goalkeeper out of position with one pass. A perfect ball. The defence re-positioned well. Shilton took up a very good position, and he's one of the best reflex keepers in the world. The fullback took up a good position on the far post. But Young's a good hitter of the ball and he hit it beautifully.

There's an illustration here of the saying that 'When forwards make forward runs other forwards stand still'; and when forwards stand still, other forwards make forward runs. The defenders had gone back with Summerbee. It would be no use the other forwards going in too; they'd have no room to play it. Summerbee took five defenders in there with him, and the forward who waited outside the box was Young. He waited and then he came on. That's why he was so much in his stride.

> **The Summerbee Lay-back**
> *(1969. Manchester City 1, Leicester 0.)*
> *Summerbee makes a tenacious run along the goal-line, slides the ball back to Young, in full stride, and Young hammers the ball with his left foot past keeper Shilton and into the roof of the net.*

★By courtesy of Movietone News, and The Football Association.

The Osgood goal, and the Charlie George goal, are excellently taken chances. Osgood's is a great header. There's tremendous endeavour in it, and anticipation. Some teams just wouldn't have had anyone going for that ball in the same situation. There's a lot of Leeds players just behind Osgood, they can only watch, but this goal isn't really the defenders' fault. This was a great ball and a great goal. Charlie George's is a good goal because of the power he gets into that shot. He doesn't really get involved enough in the game, but when the chance comes he hits them. He really hammers the ball.

The Charlie George Right Foot
(1971. Arsenal 2, Liverpool 1.)

1

2

3

4

The White Knife
(1972. Leeds 1, Arsenal 0.)
In possession just outside the Arsenal 18-yard box, Jones tries to go past McNab. At the start, Clarke is to be seen in the far background. (1-4).

The Leeds goal, that Clarke took, is the best of all of them. Here again is the principle of forwards not moving when another forward is making a run. When Jones has made his run, Clarke has waited. He's come onto the ball fast in the last couple of strides and really hit it. He possibly picked his spot —though it's natural to knock it the other way, against the movement of the defenders. It wasn't an easy ball to head, at that height; but he couldn't have chested it down, or swung at it with a high volley, because the defenders were so close. Very few people could have taken it. McNab in going down on the floor allowed Jones to get clear and play the cross, but he was a little unlucky in that the ball hit his leg in the tackle. Two defenders were almost on top of Clarke when he received the ball, and the other defenders in the box re-positioned well. There's not much that Arsenal can blame themselves for there. That's a very very good goal. It's a better goal even than I realised when I saw it.

5a

McNab goes down in the tackle; Jones struggles free. (5abc).

5b   5c

8   *The cross is pulled back, and Clarke reappears, 15 yards out. (9-11).*   9

11   *Clarke arches, dips, and snaps with his head (12abcd),*   12a

12d

13

6   *McNab recovers, too late to stop Jones crossing. (6-8).*   7

10

and as good as picks his spot between McLintock, keeper Barnett and Simpson. (13-15).   12c

14

15

Thinking of New Ideas

MALCOLM ALLISON talking with *Norman Harris*

Q: Should there be a better spirit in the game of football? Not so much arguing about a goal being scored against you, and souring the game?

A: *Well, the best disciplined players I've ever seen are the Russians. And yet they don't seem to get any really great feeling out of being successful. They show no emotion about scoring a goal. Now this worries me a little bit. I think maybe that the South American attitude is better where they get tremendous feeling into it and they're successful and score great goals. It's easy for me to turn round and say that certain players shouldn't have reacted in this way or that way, but I know the feeling out there. I know that what you do on the spur of the moment, you know, you might do out of devilment, you might do it through wanting to cheat someone because you don't like him. It's easy for a neutral person to say what's right and what's wrong.*

Perhaps it comes down to letting people be themselves and be individuals. I'm thinking of Dougan being blatantly tackled and not going mad, but just examining his shirt to see if it was all right.

Yes. Now he's a character, a good character. Good sense of showmanship. I love this, I encourage it, I love showmanship. And I think you should take advantage of these situations. It's not always possible. He was clever there. He would know that he was boss in that situation and he would laugh at it. This is good showmanship. This is controlling your mind. This is thinking about things beforehand. The seeds have got to be planted in your mind by managers. You know, if something happens, laugh at it. Big joke. Walk away. Do a little act for the crowd. Rodney Marsh will do that. Yes, I like that. But when it becomes a bitter feud and you've got to win and it's very very important, then this is taken out of the game. It depends on what's happening in the game. If you're winning and you're doing well, then you can do it — but then you may only make the other people bitter. They can get terribly uptight.

Manchester City is almost exclusively a team of Englishmen. Would a club like Manchester City beat an England team? Would they do as well if they played as England?

I don't know . . . I think they would, yes. The thing is, the greatest Hungarian team was five and six — there were five from Honved and six from Red Banner. A lot of the great national teams have had maybe seven or eight players from two teams. Definitely, co-ordination is something that's developed over a period of time. You could get hold of a team and take out what you know are the basic weaknesses and put two or three players into it and it would be a great side.

At national level, isn't it really a bit of a lottery picking a team — especially up front?

Yes, it definitely is. This is why the one thing that Ramsey did which was important, was to make it into a team, he kept them together and he kept them so close together. Now when people go on about, Bring this player in and bring that player in, it's a lot of nonsense really. I mean, a certain player may have to come in at a certain time, but people always want all sorts of players, four, five, six changes. It wouldn't be any better, for the fact that there's no co-ordination there. Basically, the thing that's always wrong with a team is it's tactics, not the players; and the co-ordination is the next thing that's very very important.

So you wouldn't make radical changes if you had the England team?

No. To me it probably only needs two basic changes in the England team to make it effective. And they would be required by the different tactics. There may be certain games, especially when you've got to win them, where you want a different arrangement of players. The game against Wales was an example. You know, there was such an obvious weakness in the Welsh team it was unbelievable, and we never took advantage of it.

You wouldn't disagree with Ramsey, or for that matter with Don Revie or Ron Greenwood, on who was a good player?

No. My mother could tell you who was a good player. You've a tremendous choice of players, and nobody would really argue that this player is that much better than the other player. It's only on that one occasion he doesn't do well — so people say, Well drop him and bring him in.

Why did you buy Rodney Marsh?

Well, I bought Rodney Marsh because to me he's the most interesting player that I've seen in English football for a long time, since Len Shackleton. I felt that if he could be conditioned to play in a certain role in a team that he would be devastating, and he's never played in that role. He's never been an out-and-out striker. And he's so cool in front of goal and he's scored so many goals, and not only does he score goals but he entertains the crowd. And his vision is absolutely brilliant. By that, I mean seeing people where they are and making passes. He thrills the crowd, you know, with his passing. I'd been trying to buy him for four or five years. When I got him it was the fourth time I'd bid for him with a definite offer of money.

You didn't seem to have a desperate need for him, though.

Yes, it appeared that way to people because I had a lot of forwards. But I bought Wyn Davies only as a stopgap until I got Rodney Marsh.

Why was it not until Martin Chivers did it that we had the long throw in football?

There was a man called Sam Weaver before the War who used to throw the ball right into the centre of the goal. It went out of fashion because nobody really worked on it. It's an unbelievable thing, you know, that it works in circles like fashion. Somebody does it, then somebody else does it—and there were two or three good long throwers before the War in English football and then nobody thought there was any point in it, nobody encouraged it, nobody worked at it. It was a boring sort of skill to practise and it was only employed by people with exceptional strength. And the people who could do it were very seldom wing-halves or wingers or in a position to take the throw-ins. The very good throwers. And you find this often today. The people who do the throwing play in the middle, like Chivers and Radford.

It makes you wonder if there are other things that haven't been fully investigated.

Television, you know, has done a lot to make people think about short corners, about free kicks, about different throw-ins. It destroys you, in a way. You try it, you do it, and people see it and they do it

The 'Chivers' long throw. It really started with Sam Weaver. "But it went out of fashion because nobody really worked on it. It's an unbelievable thing, it works in circles like fashion."

too. They'll copy it. And they stop it. You can practise little moves which you get away with for two or three years and all of a sudden it comes out on television and you'll not get away with it any more, because people are always looking for it. Long throw-ins or near-post corners, you know, all these things come out. Then it all becomes negative, and something else has to happen.

As a surprise, why not, for example, try and bomb the goal straight from the kick-off?

We do that, Liverpool do it. Wolverhampton Wanderers tried it. We've tried it four or five times this year and we nearly got a shot at goal, you know, the first time. It has to be a good ball. All you do is play a short ball and then play it back and then play a long 70-yard ball and somebody's already made their run and you try and get in the 18-yard box with it. Liverpool play a short ball and a long ball right up the touchline, trying to get by the full back in the first move.

The argument is more concerned with the goalkeeper himself. Before he's touched the ball at all, he's got maybe a 50-yard shot coming at him.

You can't get it on to the goalkeeper. You can get it into the 18-yard box and create a chance—with dead defenders, rather than the 'keeper. Actually, you would be much more successful against foreign teams with that.

In cricket, you know, the most difficult ball for a batsman to handle is really a ball bowled underarm and lobbed high in the air, descending perpendicularly on top of the wickets. It's got to be very accurate, but if it is and it's descending straight down, there's no way you can play it properly—either you hit across it and probably miss it, or you hit up into it and just hit a catch up in the air. But no-one's prepared to do that—you know, you just *don't* bowl underarm lobs like that, it's not on. But I was wondering if you could apply that to football with a very high ball into the goal mouth.

An up-and-under? Funny thing, that, I do a lot of practice with our goalkeeper, getting him to take balls at the highest point. Kicking them from the half-way line. And often I pick them up and kick them out of my hands and you'd be surprised how many balls they drop. How many they really drop. They get underneath the ball, there's no distance to run, see, and instead of going backwards and then coming in to gather it they get too much underneath the ball. You can't believe how many balls they drop.

Couldn't you just stand anywhere in the field, playing, and bounce the ball up in the air and get underneath it and hoist it like a Rugby kick?

Possibly, yes. Flick them up in the air first. You'd need a little bit of space.

The 'keeper can't get his body behind it too well if it's coming straight down.

No he can't. It's a real up-and-under.

It seems rather unscientific for goalkeepers to use the long kick

---

To throw or to kick? Jennings of Spurs shows the ball to Ritchie of Stoke.

out—just to boot the ball down the field. The opposing defenders usually have the advantage and are playing the ball back. Isn't the throw much safer and reliable and accurate?

The throw is more accurate and it will go to your own players, but the area you've got to cover with the ball, trying to build up to get to the movement over the halfway line, is going to involve yourself in a certain amount of risks. Whereas you can use long balls thrown and sort of have an umbrella of players coming to pick it up, as long as you challenge defenders. But I think there might be a little bit of a change coming now. We used to throw balls into defenders on purpose, you know, for them to knock them down and back our way, for our mid-field players to come and pick up. But we're not getting so many of them now, they're knocking them down to the side now. But with throwing you tend to risk your build-up. You get good value out of the long kick, the long ball, flighted—especially if there's any wind the ball moves in the air, the defenders don't get good headers, if they're challenged, and you can pick up loose balls from that. And also you can push your defence right up and you're all behind the ball and you push them into their own half. It depends on how well your 'keeper kicks.

In general, I was wondering if it was possible for football to be *more* professional, to get more value out of players and managers who are being paid maybe £120 a week. Is there an opportunity for doing and trying more, for spending all afternoon working on ideas? Or can you do enough and no more as it is?

This thing of working for long, long periods of time: it makes people dull and bloody unimaginative. It really revolves around the enthusiasm of the players and the enthusiasm of the manager. If the situation's there where they want to win something, where they want to really be successful—like a Cup Tie's coming up or something like that—in a week like that I can get my players to do anything. Anything. If you choose your times then you can be more professional. On the other hand you can go through all these routines and think you're being more professional and all you're doing is making the players duller and lacking in imagination. Too stereotyped, too theorised. You see this with many teams, with many coaches and managers who really work hard at it and they're really trying to be professional, but their personality is not exuberant enough. It doesn't fetch out the best in the players, and they've got a lot of boring things that they do, which are readable and recognisable by other teams and they don't bother other teams.

Do you get players actually suggesting new ideas?

Yes, you get players talking of things that they've seen or things that they think. You get players with ideas on certain things.

They presumably would be fresh if instead of the normal morning's training you just gave a particular morning to experimentation with new ideas.

Lindsay and Lloyd, for Liverpool, prove secure against the challenge of Craven for Crystal Palace. "We're not getting so many balls now, the defenders are knocking them to the side." —Allison.

No. That doesn't work. Actually, you find that not many of them do have very good ideas, you know. Certain little things you can involve them in, but they're only little things.

Are you on the lookout for ideas from outside the game?

Yes, you look at other games. Overlapping was an obvious thing we picked up, we'd never done it in soccer until ten years ago, and it came from Rugby. We started to bring more defenders back and have fewer forwards up front; have no wingers. You know, wingers create space for people. And criss-crossing came from basketball.

I suspect that you feel, overall, that football is a very instinctive game and is not suitable for the type of planning you get, say, in American football, gridiron football.

No it's not. Because it doesn't stop enough. Now, you have got to be very positive about certain things when it is stopped. Like corner kicks or free kicks outside the box, or throw-ins. You must know exactly how you've got to play, to counteract these things when you're defending, and to take advantage of them when attacking. And not to get too involved. And to try and be quick-witted and create quickly from this situation. All the great goals are scored from quick, sharp corner kicks and throw-ins. They've got it, you know, and they've played a one-two and they're in there. But you still have set plans for these things. The other team's too professional to let you do them.

What would you say if I was your goalkeeper and I came and said, Look, every time a penalty is taken against me, nine times out of 10 they score, let's accept that. So why don't we just once — especially if the game's pretty well decided anyway — when they take a penalty, instead of standing on the line, I stand on my head? The other fellow will never have seen anything like this in his life before, and the whole 40,000 crowd will be laughing and there'll be a hell of a funny noise going on. Would you say, That would be too stupid?

Well, I think you'd have more chance on your feet — that's all I'd say! I mean, all you can do is apply the average in professional sport. You know, Which is your best average? Which is the best chance you've got? You don't give away any advantage you've got. Even if it's only one-in-ten.

85

Should Football be More Sporting?

Two seasons ago there was the sensational happening of a player telling the referee that his team *hadn't* scored. The player was Steve Kember, then with Crystal Palace, playing against Notts Forest. Too honest? Some people thought so. Last season there was the sensation when Blockley, playing for Arsenal against Manchester City, seemed quite clearly to punch the ball out of goal as a last resort, but the referee thought he had headed the ball. This time, the referee was not helped out. To cricket followers, there seems to be a sharp contrast here with the way in which a fieldsman, when making a catch or stopping a ball, will signal to the umpire that the ball has in fact gone over the boundary. Professor William Barclay of Glasgow has spoken of the sight of bowler and fielders genuinely applauding a century scored against them—but "If a Rangers soccer side stood to applaud a Celtic goal I'd know the age of miracles had come". Should there be a move towards the same spirit in football? Or are the sports two totally different propositions? Is there a danger of football becoming too hard and professional? Is it necessary for the game to retain an element of 'sportsmanship' in order for it to remain a sport and to attract spectators? These questions are discussed here by a variety of interested parties. One of them is a footballer and county cricketer, Jim Cumbes. First, Kember recalls the incident at Crystal Palace.

Steve Kember

We had attacked down the left wing, the ball came across to the far post, and Terry Wharton who was playing at the Palace with me had shot in, and the ball hit a defender, then sort of hit the side netting and rolled along it onto the track at the back of the corner. Because I was following in on the shot, I went to get the ball and throw it out for a corner. Jim Barron, the Notts Forest keeper, picked the ball up and said, "He's given a goal kick." We started to protest about the goal kick, and the next thing the linesman started to run towards the centre spot. The referee had given a goal. Of course the Notts Forest players protested. As I'd been following up, I'd already said to Jim Barron, "It's a corner." He'd said, "No, it's not. It's a goal kick." I said, "You're joking, it's a corner." And so they knew that I knew it wasn't a goal. They were all protesting around the referee, and it was beginning to get out of hand. The police were beginning to come on. One of their players came up to me and said, "Tell him it's not a goal." I said, "It's his decision. What can I do?" The next thing, the referee's run down to the Notts Forest goal and had a look at the goal and checked there were no holes in the net. Then he came up to me and said, "Was it a goal?" I said, "What did you say?" "I'm in a spot," he said. "Was it a goal?" I said, "Well, no, it wasn't." You know, I thought about it, but I said, "No, it wasn't a goal." And they gave a goal kick after all that as well.

It was ironical for me. I'd got booked once already that season for asking the referee to look at the linesman. I ended up getting suspended just because I went to the referee and asked him to do something. A few lads said after the game, "Well, would somebody else do that for us?" I suppose you could say, well, perhaps another team wouldn't. The manager didn't say much really. But the chairman had a go at me afterwards. He said he didn't think I should have done it. He said I should have kept my mouth shut, just said to the referee, "It's your decision." You can argue, I suppose, that during the season there were decisions against us that were wrong, and that nobody turned around and said to the ref, "That's not really right" or "I was off-side."

Arsenal v. Manchester City. After Blockley's 'header', referee Gordon Hill—having given a corner only—is nailed at the post by irate City players.

SHOULD FOOTBALL BE MORE SPORTING?

Jack Charlton

People do protect each other. If a player gets booked for some offence and the referee thinks it's serious you'll very often find that the player who's had the offence done to him, or who's been involved, will go to the referee and say, "No, you're wrong. That was my fault. I turned the wrong way." He'll make excuses for the lad who's been booked, or if the referee looks like sending someone off, you'll get players going up to the referee and saying, "Now, come on, Ref, screw the nut, it's all part of the game." That way we protect each other.

There's no way a player's going to admit handling the ball in a situation like Blockley's. Because you get penalised, you get your name taken. It's a difficult thing. There are many times during a game where we tend to make an excuse and say, "Yeah, but things will balance themselves out over the season." It's such a fast moving game. And things like this happen so quickly that you can often be fooled into thinking you've seen something that in fact you haven't seen; someone standing just a yard or two away from an incident will get a completely different view from what the spectator 100 yards away will get. You can't really say we should admit to these things. You shouldn't admit to them. It's a game. You play the game. That's why we've got rules — to keep us playing the game within the rules. And if a way can be found around the rules, people will find it. It's always happening and always will. Cricket is not the greatest sport in the world to hold its head high. Because when you talk to cricketers, as I have, you realise they're as professional as we are nowadays. A lot of them don't 'walk', when they know they're out. One of the greatest criticisms of the Australians is that they will not walk under any circumstances. They will wait for a decision to be given, even though both teams know that they're out. It would be very nice to treat this as a point of honour, and some people do, but not all cricketers do it.

Anyway, you can't really draw comparisons with cricket. Football is dead quick and you're so involved physically, and suddenly the thing's happened and over, and you're going on to something else. If a great goal has been scored we may not actually go up and congratulate the fellow for scoring, because it's against us. But very often one of the lads, as they walk back up the field, will say, "Great goal that." They might say it grudgingly, but they will say it. And usually after the game, we tend to discuss goals and due credit will be given to good attempts or good moves that have been made. But not so much at the actual time. You're too much involved at the time to stop and think about things like that.

I've seen our kid Bobby score goals, tremendous shots, and the people on the field have just stood and looked at him. They've never thought of saying, "Great shot, Bobby, what a great effort." But they just shook their heads in wonderment — which is a fair compliment. Another thing, you'll find we're very sportsmanlike with goalkeepers. If a goalkeeper makes a tremendous save, often one of the opponents will applaud him. They'll even go so far as to pat him on the shoulder and ruffle his hair and say, "Great, you did great to get that." That's the sort of sportsmanship we tend to get in the game. And there's no greater sympathy shown between professionals than when they think somebody's really seriously hurt, with a broken leg or something that will put them out of the game.

Attention, and concern, for an injured player: a rare and welcome sight in the professional game.

SHOULD FOOTBALL BE MORE SPORTING?

Bobby Charlton

The referee is the sole judge. If he makes a mistake you don't argue with him. In any case he still wouldn't be prepared to change his decision on the say-so of one of the players. If you punched the ball out and everyone knew you had, but the ref didn't, well really you'd have to say nothing—though I've not been in that situation myself.

Football is played on a knife-edge, it's so sudden, one goal can throw you right down. Cricket is gradual. It's a different thing altogether. And there's plenty of times in football that people have said, when they've been scored against "Good goal" as they run back.

I don't think there's any danger of the sport and the enjoyment going out of football. I can't see it. Most footballers want to enjoy playing football, and they wouldn't enjoy it if the game became too ruthless. Nine out of 10 want to, anyway, and the game won't be spoiled by the other one.

Jim Cumbes (Aston Villa, and Worcestershire County Cricket Club)

Funny thing, isn't it? I've said very often to people, Why do I possibly pull a ball back that's gone a foot over the dead-ball line and swear blind it never went over, and yet on the cricket field if it hits the rope I say, Oh yes, it was a four? I think there is fair play in football, but it's a different sort of fair play. I think there is less, shall we say, *onus* in cricket to 'win at all costs'. People do want to win in cricket and there are very good professionals in cricket—very often better professionals in cric-

ket than in football—but I think they accept things far more than they do in football. Not only the players, but the spectators as well, and people who run the game, like coaches. In football it's a matter of sailing close to the wind, really. It's more emotional, you do things more in the heat of the moment. Cricket is almost like chess in many respects. You manoeuvre. Whereas in football it's all instant—the ball whacks against the stanchion and comes out and everybody says *No goal* and the referee has got to make a decision in a split second, in cricket you've probably a little bit more time to weigh things up. I think it's just a matter of speed and the emotions involved. When someone scores a hundred in cricket—compared with a goal against you in football—you've seen it coming, and you're there to see it, in a way. The batsman has probably spent two hours over it. Maybe five people have bowled at him. You applaud it. You've accepted the fact that he's going to get a hundred. You've said, Alright, well played. It's not a bitter blow. I think also in football you do appreciate it, but you probably say so afterwards though. Then you say, Well, you've got to give them credit.

But I agree that the pleasure does seem to be going out of the game. I think even now if you show any signs at all that you might be enjoying what's going on out there, the manager generally has something to say about it. It is becoming a bit zombie-ish now. If you get on with your game and you run yourself to death and you never smile and you just go through the motions of the job, everybody seems to be well pleased. George Best, even, he was probably despised in the game by a lot of people because he had the temerity to show his ability. You do get odd things, times when people joke a bit. We played in a Charity match last year against Manchester City, and one or two of their lads are always full of a few quips—Francis Lee, Mike Summerbee. But City are definitely an exception. The only time it will happen is if you know somebody on the other side. I think cricketers know each other far better than footballers do. Because we're playing together for three days.

People do try and get away with

things in cricket, but they tend to regret it afterwards. They're made to regret it by other players. I think this is the one great thing about the game. The game is always bigger than the players in cricket. I do feel that love for the game of football, as such, is decreasing year by year. You get more players disillusioned with football each year. As you get older, obviously, you start to accept it. But you do talk to an awful lot of players in football for whom it *is* a job now. It's this business of what people expect. We had it at Villa Park

Light relief with Martin Chivers of Spurs (left) and Bobby Moore of West Ham. "If something isn't enjoyed then it's a waste of time. After all, at the end of the day, it is a sport we're playing." —Joe Mercer.

last season where we played Burnley, and the crowd drifted away long before the end. Yet here they were at the time fourth in the League after gaining promotion from the Third Division. In cricket you rarely get that. You occasionally get your own side barracked, you get the other side barracked, if things are slow in cricket. But I've never come across anything like *that* in cricket.

Joe Mercer (Manager, Coventry City)
Well, it is getting a bit serious now. This is one of the things I regret about football—there's a bit of a giggle gone out of it, there's a bit of sportsmanship gone out of it, a bit of a laugh. They're the best years of your life; why shouldn't you be enjoying them? If something isn't enjoyed, then it's a waste of time. After all, at the end of the day, it is a sport we're playing. I don't think you can put these things back in by preaching. You can only do things by example, and I feel part of football is taking the rub of the green. Accepting results. No-one likes to lose, but I think there's a way of winning and there's a way of losing. You know, I think you should be modest in victory and brave in defeat. I think this is important, and anybody that plays for any length of time gets used to disappointments. It's part of what we used to call character-building, but you're not supposed to say things like that.

I remember last season, Huddersfield played us and one of their fellows pulled a ball down with his hand—took the lace out of it, almost—and side-footed it into the net. The referee didn't see it, and the linesman didn't see it. And he got away with it. Well, I was pleased the way my players reacted to that. They ran to the referee and made the complaint and after that just forgot it. But that's not morals—that's a tactical matter. As soon as you lose your temper, whether you're boxing or playing football or anything, you're at a disadvantage. It's a matter of keeping your cool. And this is our attitude at this club. We feel that the most difficult thing in the game is to get the ball. There are not many ball-winners, as they call them. It's just as much a skill to get a ball and to tackle and to set people up as it is to have Georgie Bests or Bobby Charltons beating people. So there you are—it's so difficult to get the ball and as soon as you foul, you give it away! And you've got to get it back, which is the hardest thing in football to do. This makes common sense to us, we feel.

This is the Blanchflower attitude, the Charlton attitude, the Bobby Moore attitude. There's such nonsense talked about this Jack Dempsey or 'American killer' instinct. If you think like that, you're putting power and strength and brutality before skill, technique and know-how. You've got to believe that skill will get you there in the end. It's just a matter of belief.

You've got to have a bit of philosophy to survive in this mad game—or mad world if it comes to that. But this is only preaching. You've got to do it by example.

Answers

THE TOTTENHAM PLAYERS

Martin Peters (second from right) is the only 'one and the same person'. The other combinations, left to right, are: England's head on Chivers' body, Coates' head on Gilzean's body, and Pearce's head on England's body.

THE STYLE IS THE MAN

The Dancer is Kevin Keegan, Liverpool

The Gunfighter is Malcolm Macdonald, Newcastle

The Charger is Ralph Coates, Tottenham

Pinger is John Hollins, Chelsea

The Dentist is Norman Hunter, Leeds

The Windmill is Colin Stein, Coventry

Back endpaper picture shows Alan Ball for Arsenal scoring with a penalty at Liverpool — the champions' only home defeat of the season. (Liverpool Post *picture*).